W9-CSU-865

Virtual Reality and Minecraft

By Josh Gregory

Published in the United States of America by
Cherry Lake Publishing
Ann Arbor, Michigan
www.cherrylakepublishing.com

Reading Adviser: Marla Conn, Read-Ability
Photo Credits: Cover and pages 12 and 14, ©Tinxi/Shutterstock; pages 4 and 20, Josh Gregory; page 6, ©Ken Ishii/Stringer/Getty Images; page 8, ©Tom Cooper/Stringer/Getty Images; page 10, ©izusek/Getty Images; page 16, ©LightField Studios/Shutterstock; page 18, ©Inti St Clair/Getty Images.

Library of Congress Cataloging-in-Publication Data has been filed and is available at catalog.loc.gov

Cherry Lake Publishing would like to acknowledge the work of the Partnership for 21st Century Learning. Please visit *www.p21.org* for more information.

Printed in the United States of America
Corporate Graphics

Table of Contents

Imagine looking out over the *Minecraft* world from a mountaintop. It would really feel like you are high in the air!

A New View

Are you a *Minecraft* fan? If so, you know that the game is all about exploring a huge, open world. There are fun surprises around every corner. You can climb mountains and explore underground caves. You can fight monsters and ride a horse. Have you ever wished you could be inside the world of *Minecraft*? You could see everything up close as you explore.

This VR setup uses a special controller. It makes players feel like they are riding a motorcycle.

Up Close and Personal

It's not possible to visit the world of *Minecraft* for real. But **virtual** reality (VR) is the next best thing! In VR, you don't look at a screen while you play. Instead, you wear a special device called a **headset**. It puts the world of *Minecraft* in front of your eyes. You can move your head to look around. It's like you're really there!

More Than a Headset

You will use a regular game controller to play *Minecraft* in VR. But many VR games use special motion control devices. You can move your arms and use your hands in the game. This makes it feel more real.

Modern VR technology is smaller and lighter than it used to be. Here, a real NASA test pilot tries out a VR airplane game.

A Long History

VR is amazing technology. But it is not as new as you might think. Inventors have been working on VR machines since the 1960s! Early VR headsets were big and heavy. They were also very expensive to build. They were often used to train airplane pilots and astronauts. But people did not have them at home.

Some schools use VR headsets to teach students about geography and history.

The Latest Technology

Today's VR technology is lightweight and easy to use. The simplest headsets are just cardboard with a slot for a smartphone to fit inside. People use VR for all kinds of fun things. They can get a close look at amazing places around the world. They can watch movies in a giant virtual movie theater. And they can play video games!

The Oculus Rift is one of the most popular VR headsets. It is also one of the few that work with *Minecraft*.

Getting the Right Gear

Only certain versions of *Minecraft* work with VR headsets. You will need the Windows 10 PC version or the Samsung Gear VR mobile version. You will also need the right headset. The PC version needs an Oculus Rift or Windows Mixed Reality headset. The mobile version needs a Gear VR headset. It also needs a Samsung Galaxy smartphone.

Try Before You Buy

Getting started with VR can be expensive. But you can check it out without spending money. Many electronics stores have VR headsets for shoppers to try. Some schools also have VR headsets for students.

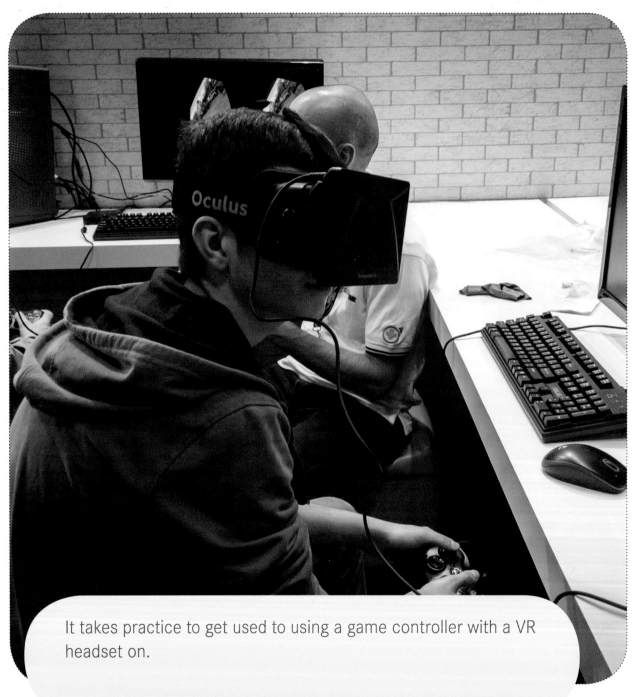

It takes practice to get used to using a game controller with a VR headset on.

Exploring a Virtual World

Your first time trying *Minecraft* in VR might feel weird. Your body is sitting still in the real world. But your brain thinks you are moving through *Minecraft*'s world. This can make you feel **disoriented**. Go slowly at first. Move your head to look around. Use your game controller to make your character walk. Avoid doing both at once until you get used to it.

Make sure your headset fits comfortably. Adjust its straps until it fits just right.

Making Adjustments

Minecraft's options menu lets you change VR settings. Adjusting them can make the game more comfortable to play. For example, you can change how fast your character moves as you press the control stick. You can also decide if you want to see your character's **inventory** and other information as you play.

Playing *Minecraft* in VR will make you want to reach out and touch the virtual world. Be careful not to knock anything over in the real world!

VR Safety

VR blocks out everything you see in real life. This means you need to be careful while playing. Stay sitting down while you play. You might run into something if you try to walk! Take off your headset if you need to move. Keep the volume low enough to hear someone talking to you. Your parents shouldn't have to yell to get your attention.

Are you ready to step into the shoes of a *Minecraft* adventurer?

A Little Goes a Long Way

Playing *Minecraft* in VR is very **immersive**. It is important not to get too wrapped up in the game. Take breaks every half hour or so. Stretch your arms and legs. Give your eyes a break. Some people start to feel sick when they play VR games. Stop right away if this happens to you. The most important thing is to have fun!

Playing the Game

You can do anything in VR *Minecraft* that you can do in regular *Minecraft*. The controls mostly work the same way. Your goals are the same. This means all of your regular *Minecraft* skills will help you succeed in VR!

Glossary

disoriented (dis-OR-ee-en-ted) confused about where you are and what you are doing

headset (HED-set) a wearable device that places screens directly in front of the user's eyes to create the experience of virtual reality

immersive (ih-MUR-siv) able to make users feel totally absorbed in an experience

inventory (IN-vuhn-tor-ee) a display of the items your character is carrying in *Minecraft*

virtual (VUR-choo-uhl) created to seem as real as possible

Find Out More

Books

Milton, Stephanie. *Minecraft Essential Handbook*. New York: Scholastic, 2015.

Milton, Stephanie. *Minecraft: Guide to Exploration*. New York: Del Rey, 2017.

Web Sites

Minecraft

https://minecraft.net/en
At the official *Minecraft* Web site, you can learn more about the game or download a copy of the PC version.

Minecraft Wiki

https://minecraft.gamepedia.com/Minecraft_Wiki
Minecraft's many fans work together to maintain this detailed guide to the game.

Index

About the Author

Josh Gregory is the author of more than 125 books for young readers. He currently lives in Chicago, Illinois.